CRYSTALS

CHERITON
CHILDREN'S BOOKS

Published in 2025 by **Cheriton Children's Books**
1 Bank Drive West, Shrewsbury, Shropshire, SY3 9DJ, UK

First Edition

Author: Sarah Eason
Designer: Paul Myerscough
Editor: Deborah Jones
Proofreader: Katie Dicker

Picture credits: Cover: Collaborate; Inside: p1: Shutterstock/Patrimonio Designs Ltd, p4: Shutterstock/Sebastian Janicki, p5: Shutterstock/Sergemi, p6: Shutterstock/Withan Tor, p7: Shutterstock/barmalini, p8: Shutterstock/Alter-ego, p9: Shutterstock/DnDavis, p10: Shutterstock/Ekkaluck Sangkla, p11: Shutterstock/Andrzej Kubik, p12b: Shutterstock/Zebra0209, p12t: Shutterstock/RHJPhtotos, p14: Shutterstock/Vvvita, p15: Shutterstock/Kartinkin77, p16: Shutterstock/M M Mustafa Soydan, p17: Shutterstock/Marcos Casiano, p18b: Shutterstock/Adisa, p18t: Shutterstock/Amanda Mohler, p20: Shutterstock/Hadkhanong, p21: Shutterstock/Albert Russ, p22: Shutterstock/IamTK, p23: Shutterstock/Toniflap, p24: Shutterstock/Photo World, p25: Shutterstock/Artush, p26: Shutterstock/Lucian Coman, p27: Shutterstock/Bjoern Wylezich, p28: Shutterstock/Photo33mm, p29: Shutterstock/Artush, p30b: Shutterstock/Everett Collection, p30t: Shutterstock/Photo World, p32: Shutterstock/Alexey Boldin, p33: Shutterstock/Terelyuk, p34: Shutterstock/EgolenaHK, p35: Shutterstock/Han Myo Htun, p36b: Shutterstock/ChameleonsEye, p36t: Shutterstock/Photo World, p38: Shutterstock/Adwo, p39: Shutterstock/Bjoern Wylezich, p40: Shutterstock/R. de Bruijn_Photography, p41: Shutterstock/Mehmet Ali Poyraz, p42: Shutterstock/A Kaiser, p43: Shutterstock/Florence-Joseph McGinn.

Printed in China

Please visit our website,
www.cheritonchildrensbooks.com
to see more of our high-quality books.

CONTENTS

Our planet is made almost entirely of rock. It has a small metal core at its center, but the remaining 85 percent of it is rock—and that's why it is so easy to find many amazing rocks on Earth.

All Change

Although the rocky surface of our planet may seem stable, it is being reshaped and reformed all the time. Sometimes, changes to its surface can happen quickly. For example, because of a natural disaster such as a landslide or earthquake. Most of the time, the changes to Earth's rocky surface happen very, very slowly—so slowly that we hardly notice them. Over a very long period, surface rocks are broken down to make way for new rocks. This is part of a never-ending cycle called the rock cycle.

Crystals play an important part in the rock cycle. Read on to find out more!

This magma chamber inside a volcano in Iceland shows **minerals** of different colors on the cave walls. As the magma cooled, the minerals in it cooled too and crystallized.

Earth's Rock Cycle

The rock cycle is a process by which one type of rock changes into another type of rock. Earth has three main types of rock: igneous rock, metamorphic rock, and sedimentary rock. Each can change into another type when affected by temperature, **weathering**, and **pressure**.

How Rock Changes

When heated deep underground, rocks turn into liquid rock. We call this melted rock magma. When rocks are worn away by weathering or **erosion**, they break into smaller pieces called sediment. Rock can also be squeezed under great pressure, which also forces it to change.

Understanding Rock Types

Igneous rock is magma that has cooled and hardened. This can happen above or below the ground. Igneous rock changes by melting into magma, eroding into sediment, or being pressed so tightly that it becomes metamorphic rock.

Metamorphic rock began life as igneous or sedimentary rock that was then heated and squeezed. Metamorphic rock can change again by eroding into sediment or melting into magma.

Sedimentary rock is made up of squashed sediments from other rocks, plus the remains of living things. It can erode back into sediment, be squeezed into metamorphic rock, or melted into magma.

Earth is one of the four "rocky" planets of our Solar System. Also in this group are Mercury, Venus, and Mars.

Look Inside Earth

To understand the rock cycle and why rock is so affected by temperature, weathering, and pressure, we need to first look at the structure of Earth.

Earth looks solid and immovable at the surface, but inside are layers that are not at all like the surface. In fact, Earth is made up of three very different parts.

Crust: This is the outer part of our planet. It is the section on which we live. It is up to 44 miles (70 km) thick and is broken up into enormous parts, called plates.

Mantle: This mostly solid layer moves around and is about 1,800 miles (2,900 km) thick. Earth's plates float on the mantle.

Core: This is the hottest part of our planet and it forms the center of Earth. The center of the core reaches nearly 12,000 degrees Fahrenheit (6,700 °C), hot enough to keep it permanently molten, or liquid.

Rock Recycling

During the rock cycle, new rock material can rise to the surface from deep within Earth. But most surface rocks are made from existing rock that is continually recycled. For example, as a rock is weathered, a grain within it may be loosened. That grain may then become part of another rock. It will then be weathered and separated from that rock, then form part of a new rock, repeatedly.

Crystals and the Rock Cycle

Crystals are solids that have their atoms arranged in a particular way. Most minerals occur naturally as crystals, and rocks are a collection of minerals. Crystals are not rocks, but they play an important part in the rock cycle. When magma cools and crystals grow, they form igneous rock.

The more slowly magma cools, the bigger the crystals grow.

Take a
Rock Cycle
Road Trip!

In this book, we will explore how crystals are created, the different types of crystals that exist, and why they are so important to us. We'll take an amazing rock cycle road trip to discover crystals around the world, some of the most incredible crystal sites on the planet, and how we make use of these beautiful structures. So, what are you waiting for? Let's hit the road and discover a world that rocks!

Chapter 2

A World of Crystals

For many people, the word "crystal" inspires an image of a beautiful, glittering rock that might adorn a ring. For scientists, the word crystal means something quite different—a solid with atoms arranged in a very ordered, repeating pattern. We'll discover why crystal atoms are so highly ordered on pages 10–11.

Crystals Everywhere

Crystals are everywhere in our world, from the salt you put on your food to the sand you walk on when you cross a sandy beach. Many rocks are a collection of crystalline minerals, and the tiny grains of sand that cover a beach are mostly tiny pieces of **quartz** crystal.

Edges and Corners

Big or small, common or rare, all crystals are solid structures. Every crystal has sharp, clear edges and corners. Many crystals have a particular number of flat faces, or sides. Snowflakes are crystals that form when droplets of water in clouds freeze. Every snowflake is different, but each has six arms, or points.

If you look closely at sea salt, you'll see that many of the pieces are shaped like cubes, with flat sides. These are crystals!

We often find crystals in caves—the crystals there have grown undisturbed for a long time, and as a result some are enormous.

Crystals from Ice

Minerals are natural substances that make up the rocks of our planet. Most minerals occur naturally as crystals, but not all crystals are minerals. Sugar crystals, for example, are not minerals. They form when the juice of a sugar cane plant is processed.

The mineral crystals in many rocks are so tiny we cannot see them. However, in rocks such as granite, the minerals are larger. Mineral crystals can only grow large enough to see without a magnifying glass if they have space and time.

The Crystal Stars

There are many crystals on Earth. Some of the best known are diamond, gypsum, emerald, sapphire, ruby.

Digging Deeper

If they have enough time and space to grow, many crystals that form underground can reach lengths of more than 30 feet (9 m). The largest recorded crystal was found in Southeast Africa. It measured 59 feet (18 m) long!

Rising Up

All magma beneath Earth's surface is constantly rising and falling. As hot magma rises, it travels through existing spaces in underground rock. It also melts new channels through rock. Once magma reaches the surface, it is called lava. When magma cools, the minerals in it form solid pieces. This is called crystallization.

As magma warms it becomes lighter and rises slowly as it escapes the pull of **gravity**. When it travels toward Earth's surface, it gets cooler and denser, or heavier. This causes it to gradually fall.

Joining Together

Crystals form when liquids cool and begin to harden. To deal with this change in matter, the molecules in the liquid group together to try to become more stable. They do so in a uniform, or regular, and repeating pattern. It is this process that forms crystals.

Understanding Atoms and Molecules

The building blocks of all crystals, minerals, and anything else on Earth are called atoms. Groups of atoms are called molecules. In crystals, atoms or molecules are packed together in a very organized way, a little like the way eggs are packed into an egg carton. One carton can sit on another because each egg takes up a particular amount of space. Under the right conditions, small groups of atoms and molecules in magma cluster together to form a solid, and surrounding atoms and molecules begin to link up, too. Over time, these organized groups of atoms and molecules form crystals that become the basis of rocks.

Rock Cycle
Road Trip!

Diamonds are incredibly tough crystals. They are made of carbon atoms that are tightly linked together. Mount Kilimanjaro in Africa is famous for its beautiful diamonds, but an even rarer and more highly prized gemstone from this area is tanzanite. Head this way for the first stop on our road trip!

ROCK STOP! MOUNT KILIMANJARO, AFRICA

Tanzanite is a staggering 1,000 times rarer than diamond. This stunning blue and violet **gemstone** is made from the mineral zoisite and is found in just one part of the world, an 8-square-mile (20 sq km) area in Tanzania near the famous Mount Kilimanjaro. The stone was first found there in 1967.

Tanzanite is known as the jewel of Mount Kilimanjaro in Africa. It is found in a small area near the mountain's base.

DIAMOND
What a Rock Star!

Diamonds are made up of just one substance—carbon—with the atoms arranged in a particular way. These gemstones are one of the most precious and valuable in the world.

Rock Star Characteristics

- Often colorless but can be many colors from yellow and brown to gray, blue, and black
- Incredibly hard and tough
- Has a brilliant shine and sparkle

Did You Know?

Large diamonds are extremely rare, and for that reason they are worth a lot of money. Diamonds are often associated with beautiful jewelry, however, just 20 percent of diamonds are a high enough quality for that purpose.

Diamonds are found and mined in eastern Siberia, in Russia. Diamonds can only form naturally around 100 miles (160 km) underground where it is very, very hot.

THAT ROCKS!

At very high temperatures, carbon atoms are forced together by the great pressure of the magma around them and the rock above them. Diamonds form hundreds of miles below Earth's surface. The diamonds we find near Earth's surface formed deep underground at least 1 billion years ago. Deep-seated **volcanic eruptions** carried these diamonds to Earth's surface.

Take a
Rock Cycle
Road Trip!

Diamond Hotspots
Much diamond mining used to take place in Africa, but mining is also common now in many other parts of the world. They include:

Siberia, Russia
Canada, North America
Africa
Australia
Brazil, South America

Growing Crystals

The melted minerals in magma crystallize as they cool down, but did you know crystals can also form when they grow in a **solution**? If you've ever watched a rock pool dry up in the Sun and wind, you may have noticed a dusting of white on the rock, just above the water level. If you did, you saw crystals in the making!

Ideal Conditions

Nearly all solutions are liquids in which one substance has dissolved, or mixed completely with another substance. Seawater is a solution of salt that has dissolved in water, for example. Many minerals dissolve best in hot water. When water trickles deep underground, it heats up as it gets nearer hot magma, which makes minerals dissolve more easily.

The Dead Sea in the Middle East is famous for its salt crystal **deposits**.

The Dead Sea has a very high salt content. As the water evaporates in the heat, the salt crystals continue to grow.

Magical Molecules

The energy in moving air and in the Sun's heat affect water molecules in rock pools. It changes water from a liquid into a gas called water vapor. This process is called evaporation. When the water changes into a gas, it rises into the air. Only the salt molecules that were in the liquid are left behind. The molecules cluster together into larger crystals as the water disappears. These salt crystals are the white substance you notice on the side of empty rock pools.

Crystal Clues

Some rocks have long veins, or lines, of crystals such as quartz inside them. These are clues that quartz mineral solutions were once trapped in cracks in the rock. Over time, the water evaporated and the quartz molecules that were left behind formed crystals that filled the remaining space.

Digging Deeper

In 1866, a **miner** drilling for oil in rocks on the banks of Lake Huron, Canada, found salt instead! **Geologists** now know that the salt deposit which lies beneath the town of Goderich, covers more than 3 square miles (7.7 sq km), making it the largest salt deposit in the world. It formed when water in an ancient sea evaporated. Over many millions of years, the salt molecules left behind became trapped under many layers of rock.

Going Underground

People who explore underground caves find some of the most amazing crystals on Earth. Caves are natural, dark spaces where crystals can grow undisturbed, and with plenty of space, for many thousands of years.

Stalagmites and stalactites create eerily spooky structures inside caves.

Cave-Making Rain

Did you know that many caves form because of rainwater? Rainwater dissolves a gas called carbon dioxide. This gas is found in air and in the soil. When rainwater and carbon dioxide mix, it makes a solution that is as **acidic** as lemon juice. If it touches a soft rock called limestone, the solution dissolves a mineral in the rock called calcite. Little by little, the water eats into cracks in the rocks, dissolving more and more of it, until a cave forms. Then, as more calcite-rich water drips into the cave, amazing crystals form, too.

The Drip, Drip Effect

Calcite droplets on the cave roof evaporate, leaving behind tiny calcite crystals. Over time, more calcite builds up around the first crystal. This creates long structures called stalactites, which hang down from the cave ceiling. When calcite-rich water drips onto the cave floor and evaporates, calcite towers called stalagmites slowly grow upward. Sometimes, stalactites and stalagmites grow toward each other to form a column.

Take a
Rock Cycle
Road Trip!

In Mexico, Central America, crystals that formed from the mineral gypsum developed into the largest crystals ever found on Earth in an extraordinary cave called Carlsbad Cavern. Let's head there for the next stop on our road trip.

ROCK STOP! ### CARLSBAD CAVERN, CENTRAL AMERICA

The crystals found in Carlsbad Cavern required certain conditions to grow. For around half a million years, the limestone caves were filled with a very strong gypsum solution. Nearby magma kept the solution warm, at a constant temperature of 122 degrees Fahrenheit (50 °C). In these perfect crystal-growing conditions, more and more gypsum crystallized from the solution, and grew into huge crystals.

These are just some of the many awesome crystals in Carlsbad Cavern.

GYPSUM

What a Rock Star!

Gypsum crystals are known for their flexibility—it is quite easy to bend very slim gypsum crystals! Their flexibility is probably one of the reasons why gypsum crystals are often found intact, unlike other crystals that are more brittle.

Rock Star Characteristics

- Often colorless but can be white or gray, sometimes red, brown, or yellow
- Flexible when handled

Did You Know?

Gypsum crystals often join, forming fishtail or swallowtail twin crystals. They can also form large, curved structures that are known as Ram's Horns.

THAT ROCKS!

Gypsum crystals sometimes form in sandy places, and when they do so sand can become trapped inside the crystals. This gives them a brown or gray color. The sand inside the crystals can also form an hourglass shape. When the crystals form in sandy areas, they can also take on unusual shapes, even becoming flowerlike in appearance.

Take a
Rock Cycle
Road Trip!

Gypsum Hotspots

Gypsum crystals are also found in other places around the world including:

A lot of gypsum desert rose crystals are found in Tunisia, Africa. They are prized by local people and tourists because they look like roses made of sand.

Chapter 3

Studying Crystals

How can we tell crystals apart? After all, there are more than 5,000 different types of minerals on our planet, and in the right conditions, each can form crystals. One way to identify crystals is by their shape.

Similar Sides

All crystals are symmetrical. This means that the faces on one side of the crystal are the same shape as those on the opposite side. This is because crystals grow in a regular way. However, different types of crystals have different shapes. They also have different ways of being symmetrical. Salt crystals have six equal square faces. Gypsum crystals have ten faces and these are **parallelograms**.

Different Shapes

Identifying crystals can be tricky because some minerals take on different shapes depending on how they form. Gypsum forms enormous hexagonal crystals in caves, but in dry deserts it forms desert roses. Small crystals of quartz or calcite minerals can grow inward into spaces within rocks called geodes.

When geodes are split open, you can see the cluster of crystals inside. These geodes contain a type of quartz called amethyst.

Breaking the Color Rules

Malachite is green, rubies are red, amethyst is purple, and diamonds are usually colorless. Using these color rules, we can spot many different types of crystals. However, not all crystals follow these color rules!

Trapped in Crystals

Emerald is a green form of the mineral beryl. However, only some beryl is green. Other types are red, pink, yellow, or blue. Each color is created by different atoms that are trapped within the beryl crystal. Emerald looks green because of the chromium in its crystals. A blue type of beryl is called aquamarine, and it gets its color due to the iron trapped inside the crystal.

Digging Deeper

Malachite minerals grow amazing crystals that are shaped like weird, melted bunches of grapes! This shape is a clue to how the crystals formed long ago. In malachite, layers of minerals containing copper form in bands around a speck of sand, dust, or other substance. Over time, many bands of slightly different color build up. Together, they form a sphere shape. Several spheres grow into each other, creating the grapelike shapes.

Confusing Crystals

Crystals can be confusing because two different types of crystal can look identical, even under **ultraviolet (UV) light** which causes some crystals to be fluorescent. We can tell crystals apart by testing their hardness. Diamond and clear zirconia crystals may look identical, but diamond can easily scratch zirconia because it is harder. Sometimes, two crystals look the same and are as hard as each other. Then scientists tell them apart by comparing their density. They chip off a piece of crystal the same size and weigh the pieces to compare them.

At a first glance, zirconia looks just like diamond.

A Color Show

Shine UV light on some crystals and they glow with weird and wonderful colors! Pink calcite crystals glow bright-orange pink under UV light. As pink calcite crystals grow, tiny quantities of the mineral manganese take up space that calcium atoms would normally take up in the calcite. Rhodochrosite is a mineral that looks identical to pink calcite crystals under normal light. However, it does not glow under UV light, proving it is a different type of crystal.

Emeralds are famous for their beautiful, glittering green color, caused by the chromium inside the gemstone's crystals. Colombia in South America produces more than 70 percent of the emeralds sold around the world, and much of them are mined in the Andes Mountains—the next stop on our road trip.

ROCK STOP! THE ANDES MOUNTAINS, SOUTH AMERICA

The mining of emeralds in Colombia takes place in the eastern parts of the Andes. There, two impressive peaks named Fura and Tena rise above the mining area in which the gemstones are dug from the ground. The emeralds are the source of stories, and in one famous tale a man and woman named Fura and Tena were created by a god to live on Earth. As a punishment for disobeying the god, the man and woman were turned into mountains. It is said that the emeralds within and around the mountains are Fura's tears!

Beneath the surface, buried in the rocks of the Andes Mountains in Colombia, are beautiful emeralds.

EMERALD
What a Rock Star!

For more than 5,000 years, emeralds have been one of the most valuable and prized of all gemstones. They were important to people in ancient civilizations in Africa, Asia, and South America. They are still highly prized today.

Rock Star Characteristics

- Distinctively green in color
- Made up of the mineral beryl with traces of chromium, which create the green color
- Often has scratches or dents on its surface, which can cause it to easily break

THAT ROCKS!

Emeralds are often found in areas of metamorphic rock. Schist, gneiss, and granite rocks are good sources of emeralds. However, the gemstone is also found in igneous and sedimentary rocks.

Did YOU Know?

Emeralds are mined in North Carolina, in a small **mine** that produced an enormous six-inch- (15 cm) long emerald that is worth approximately $3.5 million! The impressive gemstone is kept on display in the Houston Museum of Natural Science.

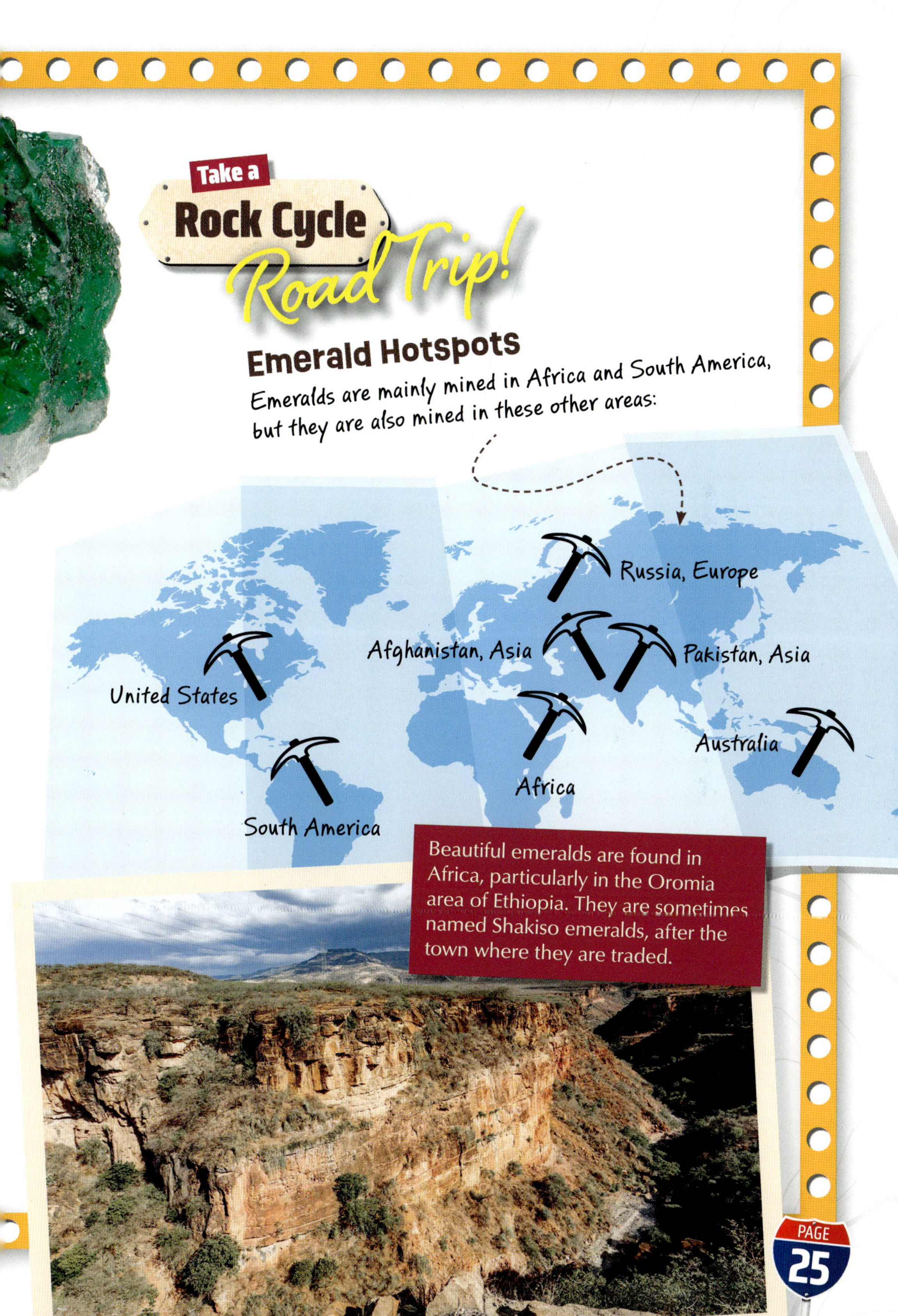

Emerald Hotspots

Emeralds are mainly mined in Africa and South America, but they are also mined in these other areas:

Beautiful emeralds are found in Africa, particularly in the Oromia area of Ethiopia. They are sometimes named Shakiso emeralds, after the town where they are traded.

Chapter 4

Finding Crystals

Crystals are buried within solid rock, which contains most of the crystals on the planet. However, the crystals inside the rock are usually hidden out of sight. Rather than break open many rocks in the hope of finding crystals, it is far better to look in the right places.

Knowing Where to Look

Geologists search for some crystals in certain types of rocks or settings. Many large crystals of rubies and emeralds are found in magma that slowly cools deep underground rather than in magma that rises to the surface and quickly cools. Yellow sulfur crystals are often found around the vents of volcanoes, because they form from gases that come out of the vents.

These mining machines are removing kimberlite in a mine in Botswana, Africa. Kimberlite is valuable because it sometimes contains diamonds.

This diamond is nestled in a lump of kimberlite, the rock these highly prized gemstones are so often found in.

Revealed by Nature

Natural processes that are part of the rock cycle can reveal crystals at Earth's surface. During weathering, hard rock is broken down by acidic rain, ice, or heat. Even tough, hard rock can be broken into tiny pieces by weathering. Erosion is another form of rock breakdown. During erosion, wind, rivers, and oceans carry away pieces of rock. When this happens, hard crystals that can resist such erosion or weathering are revealed.

Mining Crystals

Miners use different techniques to collect crystals, and usually mine where there are large veins of crystals or deposits of many small crystals. It takes time, money, and effort to mine, so it makes sense to mine where there are many crystals. Miners know that diamonds are usually buried within a particular rock called kimberlite, which formed long ago from magma that carried the rock from deep underground to the surface. For that reason, miners often search for diamonds in areas of kimberlite.

Digging Deeper

The biggest diamond mine in the world is Orapa in Botswana, Africa. It is about 0.5 square miles (1 sq km) wide. It sits at the top of two kimberlite columns, which were formed when magma from an ancient volcano cooled. Every year, mining machines dig up around 60 million tons (54 million mt) of rock from Orapa. From this, they recover around 2.4 tons (2.2 mt) of diamonds!

Tuneling to Crystals

Miners use powerful drills and diggers to chip away at the rock around a crystal vein. They dig deep underground to reach more of the crystal, so they build networks of tunnels in which to dig. The tunnels are held up by wooden or metal struts to keep them from collapsing.

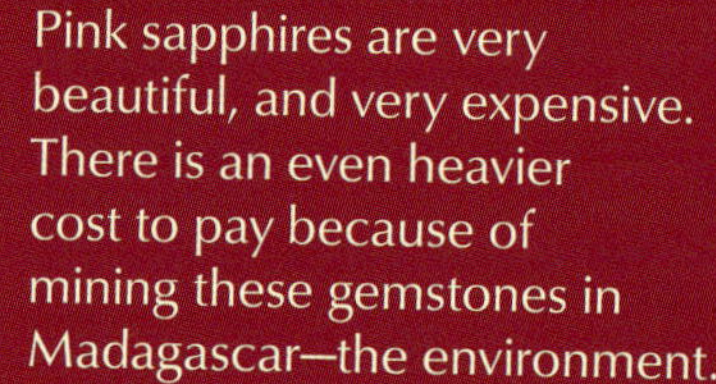

Pink sapphires are very beautiful, and very expensive. There is an even heavier cost to pay because of mining these gemstones in Madagascar—the environment.

Crushing for Crystals

When miners find hard crystals in rock, such as diamond in kimberlite, they crush the rock into smaller and smaller chunks. The diamonds are too hard to be crushed by machines, so only the rock is broken up. Eventually, the rock is crushed into a wet sludge, from which the diamonds can be easily lifted.

Swirling in Sludge

Miners find many crystals, such as sapphires, in rivers and streams. The crystals are deposited there after being eroded from rock elsewhere. Miners scoop up sludge from the riverbed in pans or baskets, then swirl it around to get rid of the mud. When only gravel is left, miners pick out the gems. Some mining companies now use machines to suck up the riverbed sludge and shake away the mud, but people are still needed to spot the valuable crystals.

Rock Cycle Road Trip!

Some of the most valuable and beautiful sapphires in the world come from Madagascar, off the coast of Africa. Although Madagascar has rich **reserves** of the gemstones, they were only recently discovered. The sapphire-rich island is the next stop on our road trip. Head this way.

ROCK STOP! ### MADAGASCAR, AFRICA

Madagascar's huge sapphire reserves were discovered only in the late 1990s, when a **drought** in the southern part of the island revealed the riches that had been hidden until then. Since then, the island has been the site of a huge amount of mining. Recently, the island's unusual pink sapphires have become very popular, and the island is now the world's biggest supplier of these unusually beautiful gemstones.

Lemurs are one of Madagascar's unusual animals, and their habitat is being threatened by sapphire mining.

SAPPHIRE
What a Rock Star!

Did you know that sapphires and rubies are made of the same mineral—corundum? The tiny amounts of **impurities** in the mineral determine if the gem is a beautiful red ruby or a brilliant blue sapphire! In the case of sapphires, tiny amounts of iron and titanium cause its beautiful blue color.

THAT ROCKS!

Sapphires are often found in metamorphic rocks, such as schist or gneiss, and in igneous rocks such as basalt. However, extracting the gemstones from the rocks is very difficult, expensive, and not often successful because the gemstones are often broken during the mining process. Sapphires are more usually collected when they have been removed from their host rock by weathering and erosion.

Blue sapphires were found at Yogo Gulch in Montana in the late 1860s, when gold miners discovered them in their **sluice boxes** while **panning** for gold.

Rock Star Characteristics

- Often blue in color but can also be almost any color from pink and yellow to green and orange. If a sapphire is not blue, it is called a "fancy sapphire"
- Hard and tough, making it a great choice as a ring stone

Take a

Rock Cycle
Road Trip!

Sapphire Hotspots

As well as Madagascar and the United States, sapphires are also found in other locations, including:

Chapter 5

Useful and Beautiful

You have probably never considered that you use crystals every single day. We rely on crystals for many of the things we use, and we even eat crystals—salt and sugar! But did you also know there are crystals in your computers, televisions, and watches?

Crystal Brains

Silicon crystals are an important part of many electronic devices we use every day. Tiny stacks of flat silicon crystals, called silicon chips, act like "brains" in many devices. The layers are printed with very tiny patterns. The patterns are a little like road maps and instructions that direct the movement of power between the layers of the silicon chips. Flat silicon crystals are also sandwiched together to make solar cells. These change the energy in sunlight into electricity.

Crystals That Cut

Some crystals are used for cutting materials. The steel cutting edges of drills, like those used by dentists to make holes in teeth or miners to dig wells deep into rock, are tipped with tiny diamonds. They give an excellent cutting surface. Lasers are machines that use crystals to direct powerful beams of light that can cut accurately.

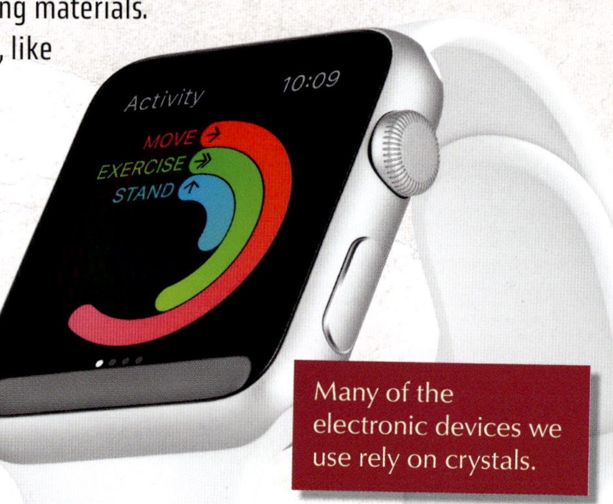

Many of the electronic devices we use rely on crystals.

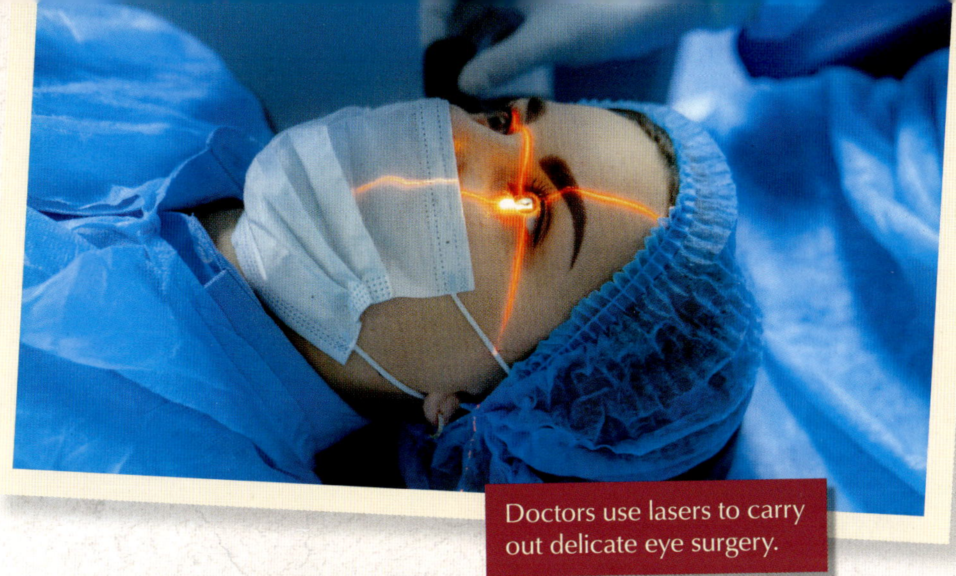

Doctors use lasers to carry out delicate eye surgery.

Making Crystals

Such is the demand for crystals that scientists make some types of crystals, such as artificial diamonds, by recreating the very high pressures and temperatures at which they would form naturally deep underground. They put tiny diamond seed crystals inside special presses that weigh hundreds of tons, together with metal such as nickel or iron, and layers of pure carbon (graphite). When the temperature and pressure increase, the molten metal carries carbon atoms from the graphite to the diamond crystals. The carbon builds up layers around the tiny crystals, making the diamond bigger and bigger.

Digging Deeper

Scientists even grow some large crystals to make lasers! They use a powder containing particular **elements**, such as aluminum and yttrium, and melt it at very high temperatures to turn the powder into a liquid. Then a machine holds a tiny crystal of garnet, called the seed crystal, at the surface of the liquid. Layers of crystal start to form around the seed. The machine turns the seed and very, very slowly lifts it up. Over time, and as the sample slowly cools, a long cylinder of crystal forms.

This jeweler is checking the quality of a cut and polished diamond.

Precious and Valuable

Crystals that are especially beautiful and difficult to find are very valuable. People buy these expensive gemstones for jewelry and as decorative objects. Diamonds, rubies, sapphires, and emeralds are among the most expensive gemstones. People set them in precious metals, such as gold, to make earrings, necklaces, and other jewelry. Gemstone workers also cut crystals into shapes to make sparkling animals and figures that people display in their homes.

Sparkle and Shine

The most valuable gemstones are those that are very clear and strongly colored. To make the most of these stones, jewelers use saws to cut a pattern of faces, or flat edges, all over their surfaces. These faces are called facets and they **reflect** light to make the gemstones sparkle. Jewelers use magnifying glasses while they work to make sure the facets they cut are perfect.

Digging Deeper

A plum-sized, perfect pink diamond known as the Pink Star was mined in South Africa in 1999. It is one of the world's most expensive gemstones. This famous stone was cut and polished for more than two years to reveal its full beauty, and then set into a ring. In 2017, it sold for $71.2 million!

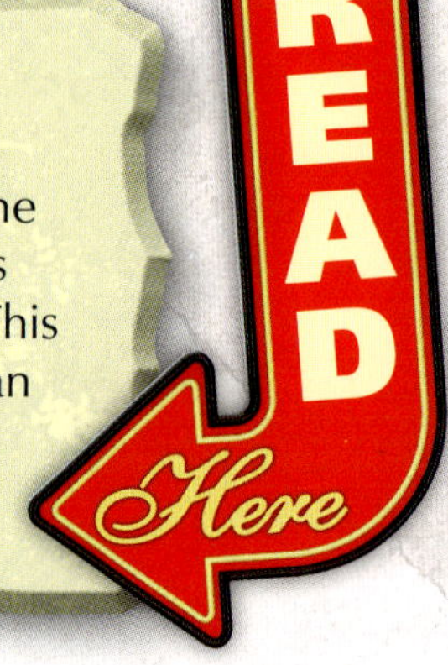

Myanmar, formerly Burma, in Asia is famous for its rubies, particularly those found in Mogok, which is a town to the west of Mandalay, Myanmar's second-largest city. It's the next stop on our road trip.

ROCK STOP! **MYANMAR, ASIA**

Ruby mining in Myanmar has been recorded since 600 CE, but mining was suspended in 2016 by the government to protect the environment. The rubies from Myanmar are highly prized for their beautiful deep-red color, and are sold for more money per **carat** than any other gemstone on Earth, other than colored diamonds.

Due to heavy mining in Myanmar, many of the rubies near the surface have already been extracted. To reach the remaining rubies, miners would need to dig to depths of more than 1,968 feet (600 m), which would be incredibly costly—both to the miners and the environment. For that reason, the remaining Myanmar rubies will remain where they are, deep beneath the surface.

All mining in this area near Mogok stopped in 2016 to try and preserve the environment.

RUBY

What a Rock Star!

We know that sapphires and rubies are made of the same mineral—corundum. Red corundums are known as rubies, and blue corundums are sapphires. The red color of a ruby is created by the presence of tiny amounts of chromium in the gem.

Rock Star Characteristics

- Often red in color but can also have orange, purple, or brown tints
- Hard and tough

Rubies and sapphires are mined in Australia. This mining is often on a small scale, mainly using hand tools such as hammers and shovels to cause less damage and disruption to the environment.

THAT ROCKS!

Like sapphires, rubies are often found in metamorphic rocks, such as schist or gneiss, and in igneous rocks such as basalt. Weathering and erosion of the rocks reveals and frees the rubies, which may then be carried away by rain into streams and rivers. There, they are often mined by hand, by washing the gravel of the stream or riverbed to reveal the tiny gemstones.

Take a
Rock Cycle
Road Trip!

Ruby Hotspots

Rubies are found in several places around the world, including:

Crystals from Outer Space

Many of the gemstones found on Earth were made during our planet's amazing rock cycle. But did you know that gemstones can arrive on Earth from space? These "**extraterrestrial**" stones were transported through space to our planet by lumps of rock called **meteoroids**.

A Sun Gem

The Egyptians called space peridot a "Sun gem" when they found deposits of it on an island in the Red Sea thousands of years ago. The rare gemstone was likely transported to Earth by meteoroids.

Riches in the Desert

The desert in Libya, North Africa, has revealed beautiful gemstones that are more than 26 million years old. Scientists believe that a meteorite hitting Earth may have **flash-melted** material in the desert on impact, creating the beautiful glasslike desert gemstones.

A cut and polished meteorite slab. This sample contains an olive-green mineral called olivine as well as the metals iron and nickel.

Made by an Asteroid

Moldavite is an olive-green gemstone that formed when a meteorite hit the part of Earth that is now Europe about 15 million years ago! It hit the planet with such speed and power that parts of the meteorite broke up and spread through Austria, the Czech Republic, and Germany. Moldavite is hard and brittle, so it must be carefully shaped for use in delicate jewelry such as earrings.

You can see olive-green moldavite crystals on this rock sample from the Czech Republic.

Depositing Diamonds

An enormous deposit of diamonds was created in Russia when an even bigger **asteroid** hit the area about 36 million years ago. It resulted in the Popigai Crater, which is the largest diamond deposit in the world. Black diamonds are other unusual gemstones that have origins in space. Scientists studying the gemstones discovered that they formed in a different way to the diamonds created on Earth. The diamonds are found in just a few places—in Brazil and Africa. It is believed they traveled to Earth as part of meteoroids that hit those particular parts.

Digging Deeper

The huge gas giant planets Jupiter and Saturn may be home to huge deposits of diamonds. Scientists studying the planets note that their **atmosphere** when combined with high pressure is the perfect environment for forming diamonds.

The Craze for Crystals

Crystals are in high demand in much of the world, but the demand can result in harm to both the environment and people. Crystals are often produced in **unethical** ways.

Mining and People

In some places, crystal miners and gemstone cutters are not paid fairly for their hard work. They also work in dangerous conditions. Sometimes, crystals are mined and sold to buy weapons for wars. However, some gem traders are working with the Fairtrade Foundation to make sure that crystal workers have better lives, care for the environment, and do not let crystals get into the wrong hands.

Mining has harmed this rain forest in South America. We need to protect the environment and Earth's incredible rock cycle so we can all use these precious **resources** for years to come.

Mining and the Environment

People need to mine to find certain minerals, but mining is causing damage to the environment worldwide. In some areas, people clear rain forest containing rare animals and plants so they can dig underground in search of crystals. The rock sludge in which miners search for crystals can wash into rivers, and spoil or block them. When miners suck up riverbed gravel in search of sapphires, they destroy fish eggs and many tiny river animals.

Crystals are precious, but so are people and the environment. We need to consider both when we mine for crystals.

Crystals Forever?

Although crystals are forming all the time, this process is very slow. We need to keep this in mind when we make use of Earth's beautiful gemstones. If we use too much of our planet's precious crystals, too quickly, we could run out of this beautiful and useful resource.

Digging Deeper

If scientists can produce crystals ethically and effectively, it could solve many of our problems relating to current mining practices and the environment. Silicon ingots are amongst the biggest human-made crystals. These pure silicon giants are cylinders that have been made up to 12 inches (30 cm) wide and 6 feet (2 m) long. In factories, the ingots are carefully sliced into very thin wafers. These are made into solar cells or silicon chips. In the future, people hope to be able to grow even larger ingots to make more useful devices.

The Road Trip
Guide to
Crystal Hunting

Had a great road trip? Loved the book? Want to try out crystal hunting yourself? Awesome! Here's an easy guide that will explain the basics. The great thing about hunting for crystals is that anyone can do it and it costs very little. All you need is a pair of sharp eyes and some resources such as books and websites to help you identify the crystals. A few key pieces of kit help too.

You can see the facets (flat surfaces) on this smoky quartz crystal.

WHERE TO LOOK

These are some of the best and safest places to find crystals:

- Pay-to-dig sites: there are many places in the United States (and around the world) where you can pay a small fee to dig for crystals. Check out the rockhound resource website on page 47 of this book for some great sites that you can explore.
- Creeks and riverbeds: these are good places to find crystals that have been carried downstream by water from their original sites. Look in areas where water flows more slowly, for example, around a bend in the stream.

Crystal-Hunting Tools

The rock and crystal hunter's most important tools are a hammer and chisel—and it's worth investing in some proper geological ones. The hammer should mostly be used for splitting stones, and not for breaking stones from cliff faces. A toothbrush and cloth are also useful.

CRYSTAL CLUES

Use these pointers to help you identify crystals:

- If you think you have found a crystal, wipe away any dirt with a cloth so you can examine it more clearly with your magnifying glass. Remember, crystals have flat surfaces called facets, which can be big or small. If you spot facets, you've likely found a crystal.
- If you are lucky enough to have found a crystal, give it a scrub with your toothbrush and some water, then dry it. Then look at it again and compare it to pictures in your crystal identifying guide to figure out what type of crystal it is.

Keep safe!

Rocks that contain crystals can be sharp, heavy, and hard, and the places where you find them may be dangerous, so it's very important to keep safe. Try to rock and crystal hunt in a group and take an adult with you. Rocks can splinter when hit, so always wear goggles when hammering. Tough gloves are useful and a helmet is also important for protection if working near places where rocks could fall.

This creek in Arizona is an ideal place for rock and crystal hunting. Many of the rocks will have been washed downstream.

The Rock Cycle Road Trip QUIZ

How much have you learned about crystals, the rock cycle, and our amazing planet on your road trip? Take the quiz and find out!

1. What mineral crystal can you eat?

2. What are the flat faces of a crystal called?

3. Why do crystals that form in a cave often grow very large?

4. What type of pattern do molecules in crystals form?

5. What two crystals is Mount Kilimanjaro famous for?

6. What mineral is found in emeralds?

7. What is special about
a gypsum crystal?

8. What crystals are stalactites
and stalagmites formed from?

9. What rock is diamond
often found in?

10. Where does moldavite
come from?

ANSWERS

1. Salt
2. Facets
3. They are less likely to be disturbed in caves and have space and time to grow
4. A regular, repeating pattern
5. Diamonds and tanzanite
6. Beryl
7. It easily bends
8. Calcite crystals
9. Kimberlite
10. A meteorite that hit Earth 15 million years ago

GLOSSARY

acidic having the properties of an acid—a chemical substance that can react with other substances to form salts. Some acids dissolve the substances they come into contact with

asteroid a rocky object orbiting the Sun

atmosphere the layers of gases that surround Earth or another planet

carat a unit of weight for precious stones

deposits places where particular minerals, crystals, or gemstones have formed

drought a prolonged period of very little rainfall, leading to a shortage of water

elements substances that cannot be broken down into simpler substances by chemical means

erosion a geological process in which material is worn away and transported by natural forces such as wind or water

extraterrestrial something that originates from outside Earth or its atmosphere

flash-melted melted extremely rapidly at a very high temperature

gemstone a mineral that can be cut and polished and used as jewelry

geologists scientists who study Earth and what it is made of

gravity the force that attracts a body toward the center of Earth

impurities substances found in small quantities in another substance, making it less pure

meteoroids small rocky objects orbiting the Sun. Meteoroids are significantly smaller than asteroids. When they hit Earth, meteoroids are called meteorites

mine to extract a substance from the ground

minerals substances formed by natural geological processes on Earth. All rocks are made from one or more minerals

miner a person who works in a mine

panning washing gravel in a pan to search for precious metals or precious stones

parallelograms four-sided shapes, with opposite sides that are parallel

pressure a continuous physical force exerted on an object by something it is in contact with. Pressure increases underground, for example, because of the downward push of rock above

quartz a hard mineral commonly found in Earth's crust. Quartz mainly contains silica

reflect to throw light back from a surface. Minerals that reflect light are shiny

reserves supplies that aren't needed immediately

resources supplies of something that can be used for a particular purpose

silicon a common element in Earth's crust, in minerals such as quartz and granite. Silicon is used to make electronic equipment. As the compound silicon dioxide, it's known as silica

sluice boxes long, sloping troughs with grooves on the bottom, used with flowing water to separate gold from gravel or sand

solution a liquid mixture

ultraviolet (UV) light a type of light that has shorter wavelengths than visible light. UV light can't be seen with the naked eye but can cause some materials to fluoresce (give off visible light)

unethical actions that are considered unacceptable or morally wrong

volcanic eruptions when gas and/or lava are released from a volcano, sometimes in an explosion

weathering the wearing away of a substance over time because of the effects of sunlight, wind, water, or other weather conditions

Books

Griffin, Annabel. *Rocks and Fossils—One Planet.* Hungry Tomato, 2022.

DK. *Crystal & Gem* (DK Eyewitness). DK Children, 2023.

DK. *Rock & Mineral* (DK Eyewitness). DK Children, 2020.

Woolf, Alex. *The Science of Rocks and Minerals: The Hard Truth About the Stuff Beneath Our Feet.* Scholastic, 2018.

Websites

Take another look at the rock cycle at:
www.cotf.edu/ete/modules/msese/earthsysflr/rock.html

Find out more about crystals at:
www.ducksters.com/science/crystals.php

Learn all about minerals, crystals, and other aspects of rocks at:
www.mineralogy4kids.org

For more ideas about where to search for crystals, visit:
www.rockhoundresource.com/where-to-find-crystals-a-helpful-guide

ABOUT THE AUTHOR

Sarah Eason has written many books for children on a wide variety of topics, from history to geography and science. She would love to take a rock cycle road trip and visit some of the amazing rocky places explored in this book.